Rita's minimalist essentials

Rita's minimalist essentials

a decluttering companion & planner

DESIGN SERVICES, LTD
4023 Kennett Pike Suite 274
Greenville DE, 19807

Rita's Minimalist Essentials: A Decluttering Workbook Companion

Copyright© 2025 Design Services, LTD

All rights reserved. No portion of this book may be duplicated, reproduced, or distributed without written permission from the author. This book may not be stored in a system maintained for retrieval of materials or transmitted in any electronic or digital form such as photocopying, scanning, photographing, and recording.

To request permission to use this material email ritawilkins@ritawilkins.com.

Quotations and attributions used in publications, articles, book reviews, and websites do not require written permission from the author.

ISBN (paperback): 978-1-7334338-5-3
ISBN (ebook): 978-1-7334338-6-0

Contact information: ritawilkins@ritawilkins.com.
Website: www.designservicesltd.com

Contact information: contactrita@designservicesltd.com
Website: www.designservicesltd.com

Designed by Brainjar Media

Acknowledgment from the Author
I want to acknowledge and extend my deepest gratitude to Elene Tierra, my amazing Marketing Project Manager for her profound insights and creative talents, and Guy Edwards of Brainjar Media, my SEO guru and marketing specialist who helped me organize and produce our newest product, Rita's Minimalist Essentials.

This product came to life because of our team's dedication and commitment to helping our global audience experience the joy of living a more abundant life with less.

INSPIRING QUOTES

"Minimalism is not about having less. It's about making room for what truly matters."
- Rita Wilkins

"Clutter is nothing more than postponed decisions."
-   Barbara Hemphill

"The space you create when you let go of what no longer serves you invites something new to enter."
- Rita Wilkins

Rita's minimalist essentials

TABLE OF CONTENTS

Inspiring Quotes i
Introduction ii
CHAPTER 1: GETTING STARTED 1
Inspiring Quotes 2
Supply Checklist 3
Decision Tree 4
Emotional Clutter 6
15-Min Burst Decluttering Method 9
ROOM BY ROOM CHECKLIST 10
Room Checklist: Kitchen/Pantry 11
Room Checklist: Dining/Family/Laundry 12
Room Checklist: Office Hobby 13
Room Checklist: Bedrooms 14
Fun Closet Challenge 15
30-Day Challenge 16
CHAPTER 2: STAYING MOTIVATED 19
Inspiring Quotes 20
Progress Tracker 21
Room by Room Monthly Planner 23
15-Min Clutter Busting Routine 35

Rita's minimalist essentials

TABLE OF CONTENTS (CONT.)

CHAPTER 3: PLACES TO DONATE 36
Inspiring Quotes 37
Places to Donate Household Items 38
Places to Donate Clothing Items 39
Places to Donate Dresses 42
Places to Donate Baby Items 43
Places to Donate Electronic Items 45
Places to Donate Office/School Items 47
Places to Donate Books 48
Places to Donate Books & DVDs 49
Places to Donate Art/Craft Items 50
Places to Donate Sports Items 51
Places to Donate Music Instruments 52
Places to Donate Eyewear 53
Places to Donate Cars 54
Places to Donate Misc Items 55
Inspiring Quotes 58
Meet Rita 59
Coupon Code 60

INTRODUCTION

>  The secret to happiness is not found in seeking more, but developing the capacity to enjoy less. -- **Socrates**

Welcome to our transformative, decluttering workbook and guide where you will learn how to go from a clutter-filled environment to a clutter-free life.

We believe that decluttering isn't just about tidying up your physical space. It's about embracing a minimalist mindset that makes more room and freedom to focus on what matters most to you.

Get ready to experience peace of mind and true contentment that comes from living a simpler life with less.

Rita Wilkins

CHAPTER 1
GETTING STARTED

Prep for Your Decluttering Journey! Here, you'll discover essential resources, checklists, clutter-busting strategies, tips for sentimental items and more. Let's kickstart your journey to a clutter-free, inspired life!"

INSPIRING QUOTES

"It takes a long time to learn how to do something simple"
- Marty Raban

"The first step to crafting the life you want is to get rid of everything you don't"
- Joshua Becker

"Clutter isn't just in our homes; it's in our minds. Clear the physical, and you'll clear the mental."
- Rita Wilkins

SUPPLY CHECKLIST

Here is a suggested supply list for decluttering. These essential tools will assist you in every step of the way, from packing away cherished belongings to deciding what truly adds value to your life.

- [ ] Moving boxes (various sizes)
- [ ] Packing tape and tape dispenser
- [ ] Bubble wrap or packing paper
- [ ] Stretch wrap or plastic wrap
- [ ] Furniture blankets or moving pads
- [ ] Labels and markers for labeling boxes
- [ ] Scissors or box cutters
- [ ] Ziplock bags (for small items or hardware)
- [ ] Plastic Bags
- [ ] Furniture sliders (for easy furniture moving)
- [ ] Moving dollies or hand trucks
- [ ] Trash bags (for disposing of unwanted items)
- [ ] Measuring tape (for measuring furniture)
- [ ] Notebook or inventory list

Rita's minimalist essentials

SORTING CLUTTER: THE DECISION TREE

TRASH   KEEP   DONATE   REVISIT

Here's a simple decision tree for sorting and decluttering items, where you eliminate four options one by one: trash, donate, keep, and revisit.

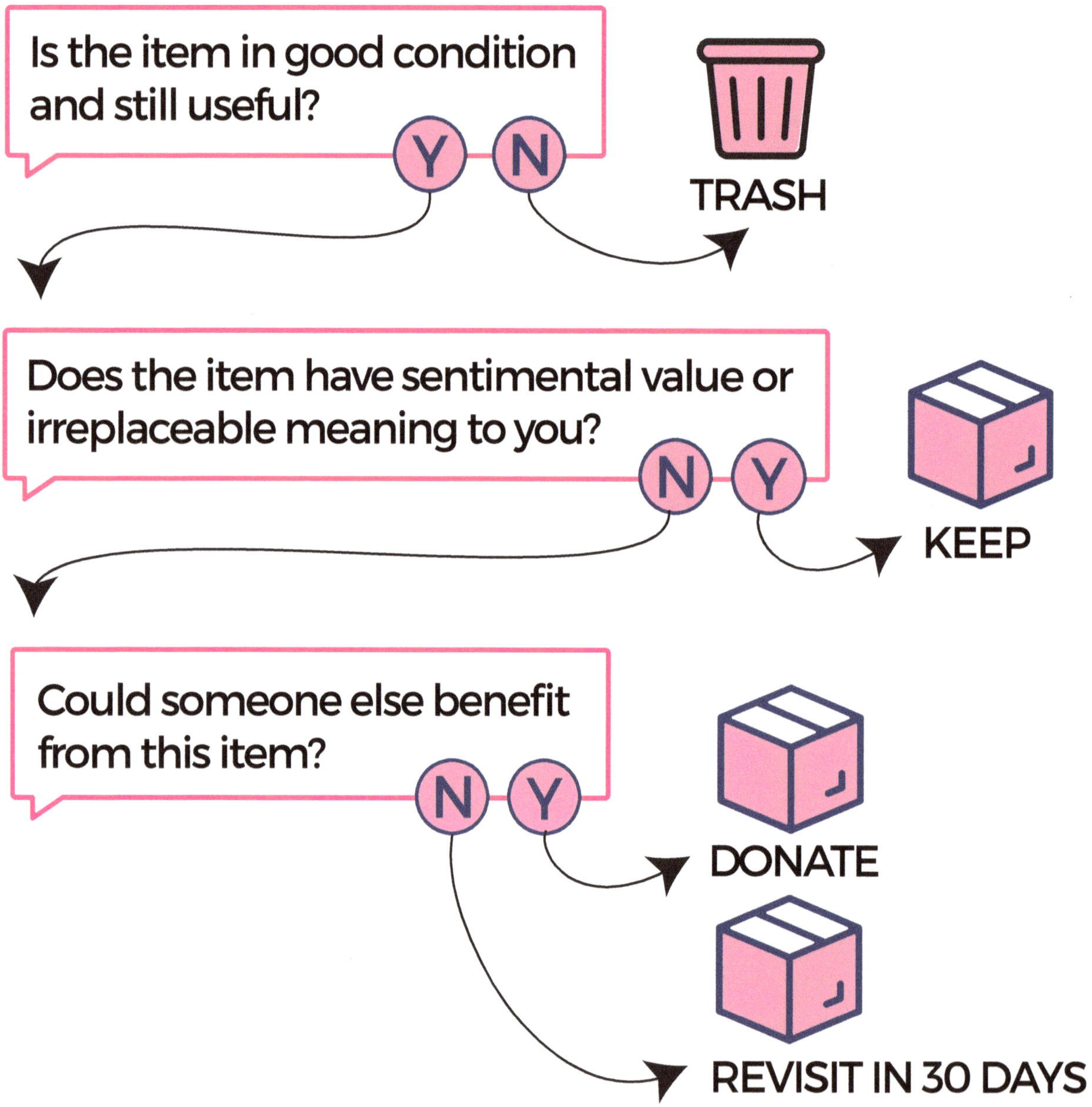

Is the item in good condition and still useful?
- Y → (continue)
- N → TRASH

Does the item have sentimental value or irreplaceable meaning to you?
- N → (continue)
- Y → KEEP

Could someone else benefit from this item?
- Y → DONATE
- N → REVISIT IN 30 DAYS

Rita's minimalist essentials

EMOTIONAL CLUTTER | PART 1 | DEFINE

Letting go of emotional clutter is transformative and healing. These two pages will guide you to free yourself, making room for new experiences and memories. Let's start by recognizing the five types of emotional clutter

Attachment Clutter
Sentimental Items Tied to Cherished Memories.
- Gifts from a significant other
- Items associated with a special memory

Inherited Clutter
Family Heirlooms and Generational Items.
- Family heirlooms
- Items passed down through generations

Aspirational Clutter
Items Tied to Future Goals and Dreams.
- Clothes that might fit eventually
- Supplies for a future lifestyle/hobby

Bargain Clutter
Discount Items, Offering a Sense of "Savings".
- Clothes you bought on clearance
- Items you bought in bulk

Abundance Clutter
Excess of Similar Items, Providing a Sense of Security.
- Sets of dishes, cups, and cutlery,
- Multiple Sets of bedding, towels, or linens

EMOTIONAL CLUTTER | PART 2 | ACCEPT

Remember, the goal is to create a living space that supports your present and future well-being. Letting go of emotional clutter is a meaningful step towards that goal. Here's how to handle each type of emotional clutter.

Attachment Clutter
While these possessions offer comfort and nostalgia, letting go brings a sense of freedom and lightness. Consider preserving the memory through a photo or passing it on to someone who can treasure it as you did.

Inherited Clutter
Though parting may initially feel guilt-ridden, it can ultimately free you from unnecessary obligations. Keep one significant item and document the rest to honor your family legacy without overwhelming your space.

Aspirational Clutter
While releasing them may seem like a loss, it can provide clarity and focus on current pursuits. Sell or donate these items to support your present objectives.

Bargain Clutter
They may seem like achievements and letting go may initially feel regretful, but it frees up space. True savings come from not acquiring unnecessary items.

Abundance Clutter
Letting go, while initially daunting, streamlines your space. Keep the best items, donate or sell the extras, and ensure your possessions align with your actual needs and preferences.

EMOTIONAL CLUTTER | PART 3 | LET GO

Need to dig deeper? Use these 5 steps to help you work through your emotional clutter and create space for a more fulfilling life.

Step 1: Recognize the Challenge
- Why is it challenging to let go?
- How is holding onto it affecting your life?

Step 2: Understand Its Significance
- Why is this item important to you?
- Why is it difficult to part with?

Step 3: Embrace Your Feelings
- Acknowledge your emotions when holding the item.
- What meaning have you attached to it?

Step 4: Envision a Lighter Future
- How would your life improve without this item?
- What positive changes could occur?

Step 5: Release with Empowerment
- A. Change Your Perspective.
  Recognize it as just an object, question the meaning you've given it. If it doesn't serve you, let it go.
- B. Reassure Yourself
  Your loved one lives in your memories, letting go isn't forgetting. Respect your feelings.
- C. Acknowledge, Appreciate & Let Go
  Acknowledge the item's role, express gratitude & release it with purpose.

Rita's minimalist essentials

15-MIN BURST METHOD: SORTING

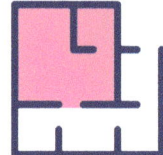    

Rev up your decluttering game with the Burst Method! This dynamic approach helps you sort through items efficiently.

If you have limited time each day or week but want to see progress, this method is your solution!

- [ ] 1. Select one small area of your home that you would like to work on. Make sure that it is small enough two complete within the time you have allotted i.e., 15 minutes.

- [ ] 2. Take a quick "before" photo of that area. This will serve to show you just how much you can accomplish in limited periods of time. It will also motivate you to try this message over and over again.

- [ ] 3. Stage all materials you will need: boxes, trash bags, markers, scissors, tape so that you can be completely ready when you start your timer

- [ ] 4. Set your timer for 15 minutes and BEGIN!

- [ ] 5. Sort into three piles: Discard, Donate, Keep

NEXT PAGE: What to do with the boxes!

15-MIN BURST METHOD: REMOVING

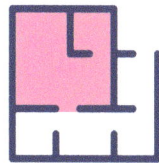    

The Burst Method continues! Now, follow these instructions to discard your items effectively and and witness a striking transformation in record time.

☐ 6. At the end of your 15-minute burst decluttering session:

- **Discard Pile:** Immediately remove all discard items from your home

- **Donate pile:** Immediately put donate items in your car to bring to the donation site or arrange for a pick up

- **Keep Pile:** Organize any items that you are keeping. Put them back so you will know exactly where to find them when you next need them.

☐ 7. Set the timer again and repeat as needed.

☐ 8. Take an "after" picture to show your progress. You might be inspired and motivated to continue. If so, select another area and repeat the process.

ROOM BY ROOM CHECKLISTS

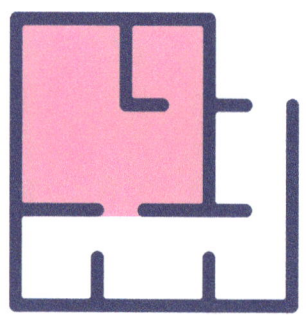

Embrace the transformative journey of decluttering your home with our room-by-room checklist. From the bedroom to the kitchen, use this guide to decide what truly matters. Your path to a clutter-free, vibrant life begins here.

ROOM CHECKLIST: KITCHEN/PANTRY

KITCHEN

- [ ] Mugs
- [ ] Glassware
- [ ] Plastic Containers/Lids
- [ ] Cooking Utensils
- [ ] Small Appliances
- [ ] Cookbooks
- [ ] Coupons
- [ ] Magazines
- [ ] Kitchen Gadgets
- [ ] Take-out Menus
- [ ] Magnets
- [ ] Appliance Menus
- [ ] Phone Books
- [ ] Junk Drawer Items
- [ ] Lightbulbs
- [ ] Warranties
- [ ] Out-dated Food Items
- [ ] Dinnerware
- [ ] Serving Pieces
- [ ] Spices
- [ ] Pens/Pencils
- [ ] Kitchen Towels
- [ ] Pot Holders
- [ ] Vases
- [ ] Cleaning Supplies
- [ ] Aprons
- [ ] Trivets
- [ ] Measuring Cups
- [ ] Cutting Boards

PANTRY

- [ ] Expired Canned Goods
- [ ] Expired Boxed Food
- [ ] Paper Goods
- [ ] Plastic Goods
- [ ] Party Supplies
- [ ] Paper Bags
- [ ] Plastic Bags
- [ ] Pet Food Supplies
- [ ] Lightbulbs
- [ ] Brooms
- [ ] Mops
- [ ] Old Batteries

Rita's minimalist essentials

ROOM CHECKLIST: DINING/FAMILY/LAUNDRY

DINING ROOM

- ☐ Dinnerware
- ☐ Crystal
- ☐ Silver
- ☐ Serving Pieces
- ☐ Vases
- ☐ Figuring
- ☐ Decorative Objects

FAMILY ROOM

- ☐ Old VCR/Old Tapes
- ☐ VD's
- ☐ DVD's
- ☐ Cables
- ☐ Remotes
- ☐ Chargers
- ☐ Video Games and Accessories
- ☐ Magazines
- ☐ Newspapers
- ☐ Toys
- ☐ Games
- ☐ Puzzles
- ☐ Board Games
- ☐ Blankets/Throws

LAUNDRY ROOM

- ☐ Laundry Supplies
- ☐ Plastic Bags
- ☐ Buckets
- ☐ Mops
- ☐ Cleaning Products

ROOM CHECKLIST: OFFICE/HOBBY

  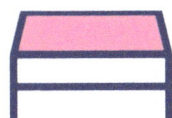  

LINEN CLOSET

- ☐ Towels
- ☐ Sheets
- ☐ Pillow Cases
- ☐ Blankets
- ☐ Pillows
- ☐ Table Clothes

HOME OFFCE/LIBRARY

- ☐ Reference Books
- ☐ Textbooks
- ☐ Encyclopedias
- ☐ Magazines/Newspapers
- ☐ Gift Cards
- ☐ Stationary
- ☐ Office Supplies
- ☐ Pens, Pencils
- ☐ Ink Cartridges
- ☐ Paper Supply
- ☐ Notebooks
- ☐ Binders
- ☐ Paper Files
- ☐ Old Cellphones
- ☐ Old Computer Equipment
- ☐ Cables
- ☐ Manuals
- ☐ Phone Books
- ☐ Receipts
- ☐ Bills
- ☐ Check Book
- ☐ Safe

HOBBY ROOM

- ☐ Scrap Book Supplies
- ☐ Arts and Crafts Supplies
- ☐ Wrapping Paper
- ☐ Ribbon
- ☐ Tape and Glue
- ☐ Scissors
- ☐ Bins
- ☐ Baskets

ROOM CHECKLIST: BEDROOMS

 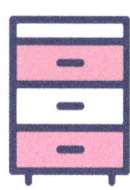 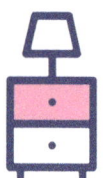  

BEDROOM

- ☐ Dresses
- ☐ Tops
- ☐ Bottoms
- ☐ Shoes
- ☐ Handbags
- ☐ Sweaters
- ☐ Shirts
- ☐ Socks
- ☐ Underwear
- ☐ Nightwear
- ☐ Swimwear
- ☐ Leisure wear
- ☐ Hats
- ☐ Ties
- ☐ Scarves and Gloves
- ☐ Laundry Bin
- ☐ Under-bed Storage
- ☐ Jewelry
- ☐ Accessories
- ☐ Suitcases

KID'S BEDROOM

- ☐ Toys
- ☐ Games
- ☐ Books
- ☐ Board Games
- ☐ Stuffed Animals
- ☐ Tops
- ☐ Bottoms
- ☐ Shoes
- ☐ Nightwear
- ☐ Swimwear
- ☐ Hats
- ☐ Scarves and Gloves

Rita's minimalist essentials

FUN CLOSET DECLUTTERING CHALLENGE

   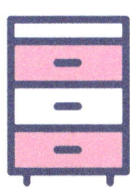 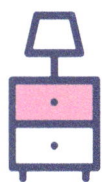

Join our 30-day closet challenge! Each day, conquer a category of quotes below, bid adieu to one item, and say "bye-bye clutter." Share the love by donating or passing it on, then have a chuckle at your past shopping spree. Let's declutter and make room for the fun stuff!

- [ ] DAY 01: "I can't believe I ever wore this!"
- [ ] DAY 02: "If only I had said no!"
- [ ] DAY 03: "What was I thinking?!"
- [ ] DAY 04: "I must have been bored"
- [ ] DAY 05: "It used to look good on me...really!"
- [ ] DAY 06: "How many of these do I need?"
- [ ] DAY 07: "Please don't laugh!"
- [ ] DAY 08: "I forgot I even had this!"
- [ ] DAY 09: "I can't believe I spent that much money on this!"
- [ ] DAY 10: "Who left the tags on?"
- [ ] DAY 11: "I must have been drinking "
- [ ] DAY 12: "No wayDAY 01: !"
- [ ] DAY 13: "It was a once-in-a-lifetime bargain!"
- [ ] DAY 14: "Why does it say "expired"?"
- [ ] DAY 15: "Maybe I can regift this!"
- [ ] DAY 16: "Definitely Secret Santa material!"
- [ ] DAY 17: "I wonder if this qualifies as a historical costume."
- [ ] DAY 18: "Why does it say, "Do not use"?"
- [ ] DAY 19: "I'm not sure which decade this came from."
- [ ] DAY 20: "Are you kidding me?!"
- [ ] DAY 21: "A gift that keeps on giving."
- [ ] DAY 22: "Too short, too tight, on sale ... I'll take it!"
- [ ] DAY 23: "Surely I'm not the only one who wore these!"
- [ ] DAY 24: "Maybe someone half my age would want this"
- [ ] DAY 25: "No wonder it was on sale!"
- [ ] DAY 26: "Wish I could get my money back for this!"
- [ ] DAY 27: "One of a kind...no wonder!"
- [ ] DAY 28: "Certified preowned, never worn."
- [ ] DAY 29: "I forgot I already had 3 of these!"
- [ ] DAY 30: "Who in their right mind would have bought this? (me)"
- [ ] DAY 31: "Found it! Best Halloween costume ever!"

WELCOME TO THE 30-DAY CHALLENGE

 In the next month (and next two pages), we'll help you declutter your mind and surroundings, leading to a more fulfilling life. Each day, explore simplification and self-discovery. Let's start!

Day 1: Describe how you were feeling right now. Physically and emotionally.

Day 2: What are you worried about or stressed about? Why?

Day 3: What would make you feel more peaceful right now? How can you have that?

Day 4: What's stopping you from having a simpler less stressful life? What can you let go of?

Day 5: List the top 10 things that matter most to you and why.

Day 6: Narrow your list down to the top three things that matter most to you and why.

Day 7: Are you prioritizing what matters most to you? If not, why?

Day 8: Describe your typical day in detail.

Day 9: Review your calendar, cut out stress-inducing activities, and prioritize what matters most to you..

Day 10: Visualize your perfect stress-free day. What are you doing and who are you with?

30-DAY CHALLENGE (CONT.)

 The challenge continues! This journey doesn't end here; it's just the beginning of a lifetime of positive change. Let's start and keep going!"

Day 11: Plan a stress-free day, schedule it, and make room by removing something else.

Day 12: Imagine the abundance of stress-free days and how they'd feel.

Day 13: Plan another stress-free day. Put it on your calendar. Remove something else.

Day 14: Identify your strengths and passions.

Day 15: How can you put more of those days onto your calendar? What do you need to remove?

Day 16: What do you want LESS in your life? Remove those from your calendar.

Day 17: Do your daily actions, goals, and lifestyle choices align with what matters most to you?

Day 18: List the areas of your life that are out of balance.

Day 19: Determine changes to achieve balance, happiness, and fulfillment.

Day 20: Set boundaries around what doesn't serve your growth and happiness.

30-DAY CHALLENGE: FINAL STRETCH

 The final stretch--only 10 days left!! This journey doesn't end here; it's just the beginning of a lifetime of positive change.

Day 21: Reframe your goals to align with your priorities, not others'.

Day 22: List 5 things you will say no to get your life back.

Day 23: List 5 things you will say "YES" to create the life you want.

Day 24: Make today self-care day. Prioritize joy and relaxation.

Day 25: Immerse yourself in one thing that you love doing so much that you lose all track of time.

Day 26: Take a nature break; rejuvenate and find peace.

Day 27: Disconnect! Treat yourself to a day without TV, News, phone, and social media.

Day 28: Have a play date with your spouse, significant other or a dear friend.

Day 29: List 10 ways you can make time on your calendar each month to live a simple life.

Day 30: Reflect on 30 days of change and apply lessons forward.

CHAPTER 2
STAYING MOTIVATED

Discover creative methods to monitor your progress, whether you're tackling an entire room or starting small with a closet. Unveil inspiring ways to track your daily, weekly, and monthly achievements.

INSPIRING QUOTES

"The greatest step toward living a simple life is learning to let go"
- Steve Marabo

"Be a curator of your life. Remove anything that doesn't bring you joy."
- Joshua Fields Millburn

"Clutter didn't appear overnight, nor will it disappear overnight. Declutter one drawer, one shelf, and one closet at a time."
- Rita Wilkins

PROGRESS TRACKER: FIRST QUESTIONS

 Transform clutter chaos into manageable milestones with this progress tracker. Begin your decluttering journey here, then let the following pages chart your triumphant progress.

TAKE A "BEFORE" PICTURE AND ASK...

1. How does clutter affect your happiness, health, relationships, mood, focus, and productivity?
_____
_____

2. How do you currently feel about the clutter in your home?
_____
_____

3. Can you identify why you accumulated and held onto clutter?
_____
_____

4. If previous attempts at decluttering failed, do you know what caused you to get stuck or give up?
_____
_____

5. On a scale of 1 to 10, how determined are you to achieve decluttering success?

| 1 | 2 | 3 | 4 | 5 | 6 | 7 | 8 | 9 | 10 |

PROGRESS TRACKER

 Print multiple copies of this page; one copy for each session. After each decluttering session, answer each of the 5 questions..

HOW LONG WAS YOUR SESSION?

☐ 15 min   ☐ 30 min   ☐ 45 min   ☐ 60 min

DATE/TIME: _____

AREA/ROOM: _____

1. Goal: What was specific goal you wanted to accomplish within the first two-hour session?
_____
_____

2. Did you achieve that goal?
_____
_____

3. If not, why not?
_____
_____

4. How do you feel about the progress you made during this first session?
_____
_____

5. Lessons learned: how can you make the next two-hour session better?
_____
_____

ROOM BY ROOM MONTHLY PLANNER

This practical guide is designed to transform your living space and, by extension, your life. By embarking on this journey, you're taking the first step towards a clutter-free and more peaceful home.

Part I: Floorplan | Mapping Your Path

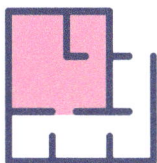

In this section, you'll create a visual blueprint of your home, from the living room to the attic. By naming each room and prioritizing them for decluttering, you'll gain a clear sense of direction.

Part II: The Process | Decluttering Calendar

Here's where you'll put your plan into action. On the blank calendar provided on the next page mark off specific dates and times to tackle each room. See sample below.

January

ROOM: Bedroom
AREA: Dresser
GOAL: Donate or trash half of the clothes

MON	TUE	WED	THU	FRI	SAT	SUN
					10-11 AM	
					2-4 PM	

Rita's minimalist essentials

ROOM BY ROOM MONTHLY PLANNER

1. Pick Your Priority Room: At the start of each month, choose the room to declutter, e.g., "BEDROOM."
2. Schedule Decluttering Times: On your calendar, mark specific dates and times for decluttering;
3. Set Phone Reminders: Use your phone's calendar or reminder app to stay on track with your decluttering schedule.

MONTH

ROOM: _____
AREA: _____
GOAL: _____
_____

MON	TUE	WED	THU	FRI	SAT	SUN

Rita's minimalist essentials

ROOM BY ROOM MONTHLY PLANNER

1. Pick Your Priority Room: At the start of each month, choose the room to declutter, e.g., "BEDROOM."
2. Schedule Decluttering Times: On your calendar, mark specific dates and times for decluttering;
3. Set Phone Reminders: Use your phone's calendar or reminder app to stay on track with your decluttering schedule.

MONTH

ROOM: _____
AREA: _____
GOAL: _____
_____

MON	TUE	WED	THU	FRI	SAT	SUN

Rita's minimalist essentials

ROOM BY ROOM MONTHLY PLANNER

1. Pick Your Priority Room: At the start of each month, choose the room to declutter, e.g., "BEDROOM."
2. Schedule Decluttering Times: On your calendar, mark specific dates and times for decluttering;
3. Set Phone Reminders: Use your phone's calendar or reminder app to stay on track with your decluttering schedule.

MONTH

ROOM: _____
AREA: _____
GOAL: _____
_____

MON	TUE	WED	THU	FRI	SAT	SUN

ROOM BY ROOM MONTHLY PLANNER

1. Pick Your Priority Room: At the start of each month, choose the room to declutter, e.g., "BEDROOM."
2. Schedule Decluttering Times: On your calendar, mark specific dates and times for decluttering;
3. Set Phone Reminders: Use your phone's calendar or reminder app to stay on track with your decluttering schedule.

MONTH

ROOM: _____
AREA: _____
GOAL: _____
_____

MON	TUE	WED	THU	FRI	SAT	SUN

Rita's minimalist essentials

ROOM BY ROOM MONTHLY PLANNER

1. Pick Your Priority Room: At the start of each month, choose the room to declutter, e.g., "BEDROOM."
2. Schedule Decluttering Times: On your calendar, mark specific dates and times for decluttering;
3. Set Phone Reminders: Use your phone's calendar or reminder app to stay on track with your decluttering schedule.

MONTH

ROOM: _____
AREA: _____
GOAL: _____
_____

MON	TUE	WED	THU	FRI	SAT	SUN

ROOM BY ROOM MONTHLY PLANNER

1. Pick Your Priority Room: At the start of each month, choose the room to declutter, e.g., "BEDROOM."
2. Schedule Decluttering Times: On your calendar, mark specific dates and times for decluttering;
3. Set Phone Reminders: Use your phone's calendar or reminder app to stay on track with your decluttering schedule.

MONTH

ROOM: _____
AREA: _____
GOAL: _____

MON	TUE	WED	THU	FRI	SAT	SUN

ROOM BY ROOM MONTHLY PLANNER

1. Pick Your Priority Room: At the start of each month, choose the room to declutter, e.g., "BEDROOM."
2. Schedule Decluttering Times: On your calendar, mark specific dates and times for decluttering;
3. Set Phone Reminders: Use your phone's calendar or reminder app to stay on track with your decluttering schedule.

MONTH

ROOM: _____
AREA: _____
GOAL: _____
_____

MON	TUE	WED	THU	FRI	SAT	SUN

Rita's minimalist essentials

ROOM BY ROOM MONTHLY PLANNER

1. Pick Your Priority Room: At the start of each month, choose the room to declutter, e.g., "BEDROOM."
2. Schedule Decluttering Times: On your calendar, mark specific dates and times for decluttering;
3. Set Phone Reminders: Use your phone's calendar or reminder app to stay on track with your decluttering schedule.

MONTH

ROOM: _____
AREA: _____
GOAL: _____

MON	TUE	WED	THU	FRI	SAT	SUN

Rita's minimalist essentials

ROOM BY ROOM MONTHLY PLANNER

1. Pick Your Priority Room: At the start of each month, choose the room to declutter, e.g., "BEDROOM."
2. Schedule Decluttering Times: On your calendar, mark specific dates and times for decluttering;
3. Set Phone Reminders: Use your phone's calendar or reminder app to stay on track with your decluttering schedule.

MONTH

ROOM: _____
AREA: _____
GOAL: _____
_____

MON	TUE	WED	THU	FRI	SAT	SUN

ROOM BY ROOM MONTHLY PLANNER

1. Pick Your Priority Room: At the start of each month, choose the room to declutter, e.g., "BEDROOM."
2. Schedule Decluttering Times: On your calendar, mark specific dates and times for decluttering;
3. Set Phone Reminders: Use your phone's calendar or reminder app to stay on track with your decluttering schedule.

MONTH

ROOM: _____
AREA: _____
GOAL: _____
_____

MON	TUE	WED	THU	FRI	SAT	SUN

ROOM BY ROOM MONTHLY PLANNER

1. Pick Your Priority Room: At the start of each month, choose the room to declutter, e.g., "BEDROOM."
2. Schedule Decluttering Times: On your calendar, mark specific dates and times for decluttering;
3. Set Phone Reminders: Use your phone's calendar or reminder app to stay on track with your decluttering schedule.

MONTH

ROOM: _____
AREA: _____
GOAL: _____
_____

MON	TUE	WED	THU	FRI	SAT	SUN

Rita's minimalist essentials

15-MIN CLUTTER BUSTING ROUTINE

Keep up the minimalist momentum and prevent future clutter by making this short routine a habit, you'll inspire loved ones to join in, creating a positive ripple effect. Embrace the change and enjoy the benefits!

1. Recognize Your "Dumping Grounds"
- ☐ List your common clutter hotspots (e.g., kitchen counter, bathroom vanity, your desktop).
- ☐ Develop the habit of immediate storage, returning items to their designated spots.

2. Tackle Piling Items
- ☐ Promptly address items prone to piling up (e.g., junk mail, magazines, dirty clothing).
- ☐ Prevent accumulation by taking swift action (e.g., recycling junk mail, donating old magazines).

3. Overcome Procrastination
- ☐ Identify tasks you often postpone (e.g., making your bed, doing the dishes, putting away clothing).
- ☐ Embrace the "DO IT NOW" mantra, experience reduced stress, increased peace of mind, and enhanced organization.

4. Locate What You Can't Find
- ☐ Identify frequently misplaced items (e.g., phone, remote control, glasses, keys).
- ☐ Establish designated "homes" for these items and cultivate a habit of returning them after use.

CHAPTER 3
PLACES TO DONATE

100 Donation Destinations! From small items to clothing, electronics, furniture, and even cars, we've got you covered with a wealth of nspiring donation options.

INSPIRING QUOTES

"The things you own end up owning you."
- Chuck Palahniuk

"Simplicity is the keynote of all true elegance.."
- Coco Chanel

"Your home is living space, not storage space."
- Rita Wilkins

PLACES TO DONATE: HOUSEHOLD ITEMS

☐ 1. ENCORE SHOP: https://www.chestercountyhospital.org/giving/get-involved/shopwith-purpose/the-encore-shop

What they do: Our philosophy is to offer quality merchandise for resale.

What they need: Clothing, furniture, jewelry

☐ 2. MINISTRY OF CARING: https://www.ministryofcaring.org/

What they do: a vibrant community of staff, volunteers, donors and diverse supporters united by a passion to serve the poor.

What they need: new or lightly used clothing for the poor is always appreciated. So are new toilet articles and other household items and furniture in good condition.

☐ 3. GOODWILL: http://www.goodwill.org/

What they do: Help people with barriers to employment learn skills to find competitive employment.

What they need: Clothing, electronics, appliances, furniture and more.

☐ 4. SALVATION ARMY: https://www.salvationarmyusa.org/usn/

What they do: Provide community programs, homeless services, rehabilitation, disaster relief and other assistance to those in need.

What they need: Clothing, furniture, household goods, sporting equipment, books, electronics, and more.

☐ 5. VIETNAM VETERANS OF AMERICA: https://vva.org/

What they do: Help Vietnam-era veterans and their families.

What they need: clothing, baby items, housewares, electronics, small appliances, tools and just about anything else

PLACES TO DONATE: HOUSEHOLD ITEMS

☐ 6. VOLUNTEERS OF AMERICA: https://www.voa.org/

What they do: Support at-risk youth, the frail elderly, men and women returning from prison, homeless individuals and families, people with disabilities, and those recovering from addictions.

What they need: clothing, furniture toys, and household goods for their thrift stores.

☐ 7. CAUSE USA: https://cause-usa.org/

What they do: Send gift packs to wounded military personnel and their families.

What they need: Playing cards, handheld electronic games, current magazines, batteries, travel-size toiletries, and more.

☐ 8. THE ARC: TheArc.org

What they do: They have been supporting individuals with intellectual and developmental disabilities since 1950.

What they need: Furniture and houseware, clothing and shoes, electronics, toy andgames, used cars and books.

☐ 9. AMVETS NATIONAL SERVICVE FOUNDATION: https://amvets.org/

What they do: Supports U.S. war veterans, both active duty servicemen and woman and those who honorably discharged.

What they need: Small furniture and appliances, clothing and accessories, toys and games, electronics, bedding, bicycles and more.

PLACES TO DONATE: CLOTHING, ETC.

   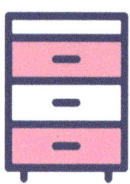 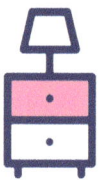

☐ 10. ONE WARM COAT: https://www.onewarmcoat.org/

What they do: Provide free coats to people in need.
What they need: Coats, jackets, fleece, and warmers.

☐ 11. PLANET AID: https://www.planetaid.org/

What they do: They recycle clothes and shoes in a yellow Planet Aid bin and provide it to people who needs it most.
What they need: Used clothes, shoes, and textiles

☐ 12. SCHOOLA: https://www.schoola.com/how-it-works

What they do: Their unique fundraising solutions turns clothing into money for your kid's school. You can also track your school's fundraising progress online. What they need: Clothes from home

13. DELAWARE BREAST CANCER COALLITION | GREAT STUFF SAVVY RESALE: http://greatstuffresale.com/

What they do: The shop offers a variety of high quality items, including women's clothing, shoes, and jewelry. We also have a section for designer clothing, evening wear, business attire, and petites.
What they need: High quality women's clothing, shoes, accessories, furniture and decorative items.

☐ 14. BEEBEE'S TREASURE CHEST THRIFT SHOP: https://www.beebehealthcare.org/make-gift/thrift-shop

What they do: a fundraising success for Beebe Healthcare, aiding the Beebe Auxiliary in lit's tireless effort to support the healthcare that it brings to the community. What they need: Men, women, and children's clothing

15. DESIGNERS CONSIGNER: http://designerconsignerde.com/

What they do: Delaware's premier upscale resale boutique, packed full of all the brandsyou want, at prices you'll LOVE! What they need: Upscale designer clothing and accessories for men and women

PLACES TO DONATE: CLOTHING, ETC.

   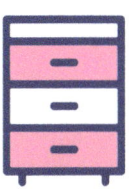 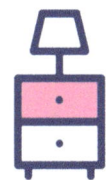

☐ **26. DIAMONDS FOR DREAMS:**
https://www.makingmemories.org/diamonds_for_dreams.html

What they do: The donations will be sold with profits granting wishes for terminal breast cancer patients.
What they need: diamond jewelries and other special jewelry items.

☐ **27. ANIMAL GUARDING NETWORK:** https://animalguardiannetwork.org

What they do: Using their eBay store, they sell all donations. 100% of their proceeds go to help animals in their shelter.
What they need: Used jewelry and accessories.

PLACES TO DONATE: DRESSES

- [ ] **28. THE GIVING GOWN:** https://www.givinggown.org/

  What they do: They promote confidence and self-esteem to high school girls and help them attend their formal events in style, regardless of financial circumstances.
  What they need: Gowns, dresses, and accessories.

- [ ] **29. BRIDES AGAINST BREAST CANCER:** https://www.bridesagainstbreastcancer.org/

  What they do: Advance the awareness of breast cancer, and operate a wish-granting service enabling patients to make special memories with their loved ones.
  What they need: new and used wedding gowns from 2005 to present.

- [ ] **30. BRIDES ACROSS AMERICA:** https://www.bridesacrossamerica.com/

  What they do: Provide wedding gowns to military brides in need
  What they need: New or gently-used bridal gowns, not more than three years old.

- [ ] **31. GLASS SLIPPER PROJECT:** https://www.glassslipperproject.org/

  What they do: Collect formal dresses and accessories and provide them, free of charge, to students who are unable to purchase their own prom attire.
  What they need: New and almost-new prom dresses and accessories.

- [ ] **32. OPERATION PROM:** https://operationprom.org/donate.php

  What they do: They help teenagers who cannot afford to get their prom dresses and suits.
  What they need: Dresses and tuxedos

PLACES TO DONATE: BABY & KID ITEMS

☐ 33. SECOND CHANCE TOYS: https://www.secondchancetoys.org/

What they do: Keeping plastic toys out of landfills by donating them to children in need.
What they need: Children toys and other children items.

☐ 34. PROJECT NIGHT NIGHT: http://www.projectnightnight.org/

What they do: Reduce the trauma of homeless children with Night Night Packages or childhood comforts.
What they need: stuffed animals, blankets, and children's books

☐ 35. SAFE (STUFFED ANIMALS FOR EMERGENCIES): https://stuffedanimalsforemergencies.org/

What they do: collect items to give to children in emotional, traumatic, or stressful situations (like fires, illness, abuse, homelessness and natural disasters)
What they need: New or gently-used stuffed animals

☐ 36. PROJECT SMILE: http://www.projectsmile.org/
What they do: Provide emergency responders with children's comfort items, to help ease their pain and fear
What they need: New or gently-used stuffed animals, children's books, unused coloring books, new crayons

PLACES TO DONATE: BABY & KID ITEMS

☐ **37. NEWBORNS IN NEED: https://newbornsinneed.org/**

What they do: Provide care necessities to local agencies and hospitals serving premature, ill, or impoverished newborns.
What they need: Baby clothing, toys, and other items; also, fabric, yarn, thread and other supplies.

☐ **38. RONALD MCDONALD HOUSE: https://www.rmhc.org/**

What they do: Provide a "home-away-from-home" for families so they can stay close by their hospitalized child at little or no cost.
What they need: New toys, food and household products.

☐ **39. TOYS FOR TOTS: https://www.toysfortots.org/donate/toys.aspx**

What they do: Toys collected and given to unprivileged kids as Christmas presents.
What they need: Any children toys that are in good condition.

☐ **40. NATIONAL CENTER FOR CHILDREN IN POVERTY: https://www.nccp.org/**

What they do: They aim to improve the lives of low-income children and their families by delivering our research to advocates and policymakers seeking to craft effective policies that promote healthy child development, and strong, nurturing families that are economically secure.
What they need: Any children items.

PLACES TO DONATE: ELECTRONICS

- [ ] **41. COMPUTERS WITH CAUSES:** https://www.computerswithcauses.org/computerdonations.htm

    What they do: Their goal is to provide a refurbished computer gifted by our generous donors towards an educational, future learning program, foster home or disabled veteran in need.
    What they need: Laptops, tablets, desktop servers or other miscellaneous tech gadgets.

- [ ] **42. HELPLINE FROM VERIZON:** http://www.verizonwireless.com/

    What they do: Donations will be distributed to domestic violence organizations. You cansend it to them or drop your donations off in a store.
    What they need: Old mobile phones.

- [ ] **43. NATIONAL COALITION AGAINS DOMESTIC VIOLENCE:** https://ncadv.org/donate-a-phone

    What they do: Donations go directly to furthering NCADV's programming and projects that support victims and survivors of domestic violence and the advocates and allies that support them.
    What they need: Any cell phone in any condition and their accessories, laptops, Mp3 players, digital cameras and more.

- [ ] **44. WORLD COMPUTER EXCHANGE:** https://worldcomputerexchange.org/
    What they do: Provide used computers and technology to schools, libraries, community centers and universities
    What they need: Computers, laptops, printers, hard drives, software and more.

- [ ] **45. NATIONAL CHRISTINA FOUNDATION:** http://www.ncadv.org/
    What they do: Work to eliminate domestic violence, and empower battered women and children.
    What they need: Used cell phones.

Rita's minimalist essentials

PLACES TO DONATE: ELECTRONICS

☐ **46. COMPUTER RECYCLING CENTER:** https://its.temple.edu/lab/computerrecycling-center

What they do:
Place computer in public charity and community programs through Computers & Education ™, and recycle unusable items to keep them out of landfills.
What they need: Computers, laptops, home electronics

☐ **47. CELLPHONES FOR SOLIDERS:** https://www.cellphonesforsoldiers.com/

What they do: Use the money from recycling cell phones to purchase calling cards fortroops in need
What they need: used cell phones.

☐ **48. HOMEBOY RECYCLING:** https://homeboyrecycling.com/

What they do: We demanufacture electronics at the end of their useful life, recovering the metals, plastics, and other materials they consist of.
What they need: Any electronics that you are to dispose of.

PLACES TO DONATE: OFFICE/SCHOOL

☐ **49. MUSCULAR DYSTROPHY FOUNDATION:** https://www.mda.org/

What they do: Fund worldwide research efforts and nationwide programs to aid with neuromuscular diseases and their families.
What they need: Computers, software, office equipment, furniture and supplies for use in
local offices.

☐ **50. DEVELOP AFRICA:** https://www.developafrica.org/

What they do: Provide books, schools and teaching supplies, scholarships, and job-related training in Africa.
What they need: A wide variety of school and office supplies

PLACES TO DONATE: BOOKS

☐ **51. BETTER WORLD BOOKS:** https://services.betterworldbooks.com/individuals/

What they do: Each sale generates funds for literacy and education initiatives in the UK, US and around the world.
What they need: Any gently used books

☐ **52. INTERNATIONAL BOOK PROJECT:** https://www.intlbookproject.org/

What they do: Promote education and literacy by sending quality used books overseas.
What they need: Textbooks, dictionaries, encyclopedias, vocational books, children's books and more.

☐ **53. BOOKS FOR AFRICA:** https://www.booksforafrica.org/

What they do: Help create a culture of literacy by shipping books to libraries and classrooms in Africa.
What they need: A wide variety of new and gently-used.

☐ **54. THE BRIDGE OF BOOKS FOUNDATION:** https://bridgeofbooksfoundation.org/

What they do: Provide books to children in low-income families, particularly through foster family agencies, homeless shelters, underfunded schools, and neighborhood centers.
What they need: new and used children's books, from preschool through high school

☐ **55. BOOKS THROUGH BARS:** http://booksthroughbars.org/

What they do: Send quality reading and educational material to prisoners, thereby promoting successful community re-integration.
What they need: A variety of new and gently-used books. Please email before shipping.

PLACES TO DONATE: BOOKS

☐ 56. BOOKS FOR SOLIDERS: http://booksforsoldiers.com/

What they do: Facilitate the direct donation of books to soldiers serving overseas.
What they need: Books and magazines (as well as CDs, DVDs and video games) requested by soldiers.

☐ 57. OPERATION PAPERBACK: https://www.operationpaperback.org/

What they do: Volunteers collect gently-used books and send them to American troops overseas, as well as veterans and military families here at home.
What they need: Gently used books

PLACES TO DONATE: DVDs & CDs

☐ 58. DVDS4VETS: http://dvds4vets.org/

What they do: All donations are to be given as entertainment for veterans who are unable to obtain movies on their own.
What they need: DVDs, blu-rays and players

☐ 59. KID FLICKS: http://www.kidflicks.org/

What they do: Create movie libraries for children's hospitals and pediatric wards across the U.S.
What they need: DVDs

☐ 60. MUSICIANS ON CALL: https://www.musiciansoncall.org/

What they do: Provide hospitals with complete CD libraries and players for patient use
What they need: New or gently-used CDs and new/unused personal CD players

PLACES TO DONATE: CRAFT SUPPLIES

☐ 61. BINKY PATROL: https://binkypatrol.org/
What they do: Distribute homemade blankets (sewn, knitted, crocheted, or quilted) to children in need
What they need: Fabric, yarn, batting and finished blankets

☐ 62. MANY ARMS REACH YOU: http://www.manyarms.org/
What they do: Collect and donate knitted, quilted or crocheted blankets to disadvantaged mothers and their children.
What they need: Yarn

☐ 63. THE MOTHER BEAR PROJECT: http://motherbearproject.org/
What they do: Provide hand-knit and crocheted bears to children with HIV/AIDS in emerging nations.
What they need: Yarn, knitting needles, PolyFill, postage stamps, packing tape

☐ 64. KNOTS OF LOVE: http://www.knotsoflove.org/
What they do: Provide crocheted and knitted caps for chemo patients and others facinglife-threatening illnesses and injuries.
What they need: Yarn

☐ 65. MADE 4 AID: http://www.made4aid.org/
What they do: Sell handmade items on Etsy to raise funds for Doctors Without Borders
What they need: A variety of handmade items, as well as arts and crafts material.

☐ 66. CARE WEAR: http://www.carewear.org/
What they do: Care wear is a nationwide group of volunteers who knit, crochet, and/orsew, providing handmade items directly to hospitals and social services agents.
What they need: Extra yarn or knitting supplies.

☐ 67. THE DREAMING ZEBRA: https://dreamingzebra.org/index.php/getinvolved/send-your-supplies
What they do: They help underprivileged children experience the joy of making art.
What they need: Art supplies like paint, brushes, markers, clay and even musical Instruments.

PLACES TO DONATE: SPORTS EQUIP.

☐ **68. SPORTS GIFT:** http://www.sportsgift.org/

What they do: Provide sports programs and equipment to impoverished and disadvantaged children throughout the world.
What they need: A wide variety of sports equipment.

☐ **69. ONE WORLD RUNNING:** http://oneworldrunning.com/

What they do: provide running shoes to those in need in the US and throughout theworld.
What they need: New and near-new running shoes

☐ **70. BIKES FOR THE WORLD:** https://www.bikesfortheworld.org/

What they do: Donate bicycles to developing countries, so that individuals can get to work or school, or provide health and education services to low-income rural people.
What they need: Any serviceable adult or children's bicycles, as well as bike parts, tools and accessories

☐ **71. BICYCLES FOR HUMANITY:** http://bicycles-for-humanity.org/

What they do: Send bicycles to developing countries, to empower disadvantaged people through improved access to food and water, employment, healthcare, education and social opportunities.
What they need: bicycles, as well as, bike parts, tools, clothing, helmets, tires, and tubes

☐ **72. PEACE PASSERS:** http://peacepassers.org/

What they do: Distribute soccer supplies to communities in need, to empower youth and maximize hope.
What they need: soccer gear like balls, shoes, jerseys, shorts, and socks.

PLACES TO DONATE: MUSIC

- [ ] **73. HUNGRY FOR MUSIC:** https://hungryformusic.org/

  What they do: They serve children who demonstrate a desire to learn music, as well as teachers who have students willing to learn.
  What they need: Any musical instrument

- [ ] **74. MR. HOLLAND'S OPUS FOUNDATION:** https://www.mhopus.org/

  What they do: Keep music alive in our schools and communities by donating musical instruments to under-Gently-used band or orchestral instruments

- [ ] **75. EDUCATION THROUGH MUSIC:** https://etmonline.org/

  What they do: Promote the integration of music into the curricula of disadvantaged schools in order to enhance student' academic performance and general development.
  What they need: A variety of musical instruments

PLACES TO DONATE: EYEWEAR

- [ ] 76. SIGHT: https://sight.org/

  What they do: Donate your used eyeglasses and they will prescribe them to someone in Togo, West Africa, who would greatly benefit from them!
  What they need: Used eyeglasses

- [ ] 77. UNITE FOR SIGHT: https://www.uniteforsight.org/

  What they do: Support eye care for patients living in extreme poverty in developing countries
  What they need: new reading glasses, distance glasses and sunglasses

- [ ] 78. ONE SIGHT: https://onesight.org/

  What they do: Provide free vision care and eyewear to people in need around the world
  What they need: Gently-used eyewear

- [ ] 79. NEW EYES FOR THE NEEDY: https://www.new-eyes.org/

  What they do: Send eyeglasses to medical missions and international charitable organizations for distribution to the poor in developing nations.

- [ ] 80. LION'S CLUB: https://www.lionsclubs.org/en

  What they do: Vision screening for children and vision support group.
  What they need: Monetary donations or used eyeglasses.

PLACES TO DONATE: CARS

☐ 81. CAR TALK: https://www.cartalk.com/car-donation/

What they do: Their goal is to assess each car donated and find a way to get the maximum donation for your station.
What they need: Cars, trucks, boats, planes, motorcycles, RVs, and heavy equipment, running or not.

☐ 82. DONATE A CAR: https://www.donateacar.com/

What they do: This website allows you to find charities in your area that accepts cars as a donation.
What they need: Used cars

☐ 83. DAV: https://www.dav.org/vehicle-donation/

What they do: Helping a veteran in need for vehicle. Fill out their questionnaire with the make, model and vehicle information and they will instruct you with the best way to donate your car.
What they need: All types of vehicles

☐ 84. CARS FOR KID'S SAKE: http://www.bbbs.org/cars-for-kids-sake/

What they do: Donate unwanted vehicles (all kins) to be sold. The profits benefits Big Brother Big Sisters Foundation.
What they need: All types of vehicles, including cars, trucks, SUVs, motor homes, boats, airplanes, farm equipment, and construction equipment.

☐ 85. KARS4KIDS: https://www.kars4kids.org/

What they do: Their vision is to give our children the ability to succeed in life. We focuson educational, mentorship and year-round programs for our children, their families and their communities. We rely on thousands of volunteers.
What they need: Any type of car/vehicle

PLACES TO DONATE: CARS

☐ 86. BIG BROTHERS BIG SISTERS CARS FOR KIDS SAKE: https://www.bbbs.org/cars-for-kids-sake/

What they do: Provide children facing adversity with strong and enduring, professionally supported one-to-one relationships that change their lives for the better.
What they need: All types of vehicles, including cars, trucks, SUVs, motor homes, boats, airplanes, farm equipment, and construction equipment.

☐ 87. HABITAT FOR HUMANITY CARS FOR HOMES: https://www.habitat.org/support/how-to-donate-your-car

What they do: build and rehabilitate houses for families in need
What they need: cars, trucks, boats, RVs, motorcycles, and construction equipment

☐ 88. NATIONAL KIDNEY FOUNDATION KIDNEY CARS: https://www.kidney.org/support/kidneycars

What they do: Fund public health and professional education, vital patient and community services, organ donation programs and medical research to prevent kidney disease.
What they need: Cars, vans, trucks, and boats

☐ 89. PURPLE HEART: https://cardonation.purpleheartcars.org/

What they do: provide a variety of programs for wounded and disabled veterans and their families.
What they need: cars, trucks, RVs and boats

☐ 90. THE SALVATION ARMY: https://satruck.org/vehicle/create

What they do: When you donate goods to The Salvation Army, those items are then sold at their Thrift Stores and the proceeds are used to fund their Adult Rehabilitation Centers, where those struggling with drugs and alcohol fin d help, hope, and a second chance at life.

Rita's minimalist essentials

PLACES TO DONATE: MISCELLANEOUS

☐ 91. NATIONAL FURNITURE BANK: http://furniturebanks.org/

What they do: Provide beds, tables, chairs, and other crucial home furnishing to over 100,000 people in need each year.
What they need: Beds, dressers, nightstands, tables, chairs, sofas, lamps, and more.

☐ 92. ST. JUDE'S RANCH: https://stjudesranch.org/recycled-card-program/

What they do: Serve all abused, abandoned, and neglected children and families in a safe, homelike environment.
What they need: Used greeting cards

☐ 93. PICKUPMYDONATION.COM: https://www.pickupmydonation.com/

What they do: assists non-profit thrift stores in your area with securing items they may need for their own operations or those who they are helping.
What they need: Large items that can't be easily be donated without a truck.

☐ 94. HABITAT FOR HUMANITY RESTORE: https://www.habitat.org/restores/donategoods

What they do: Their proceed go towards providing homes for underprivilege families.
What they need: Clothing, furniture, household goods, appliances, automobiles. What they need: New and gently used appliance, furniture, building material and household goods.

☐ 95. SOLES 4 SOULS: https://soles4souls.org/give-shoes/

What they do: They help people in developing countries launch and sustain their own small businesses selling donated shoes and clothing. Give them the opportunity to break free from the cycle of poverty.
What they need: Used shoes and clothing.

PLACES TO DONATE: MISCELLANEOUS

- [ ] **96. GIVE A BACK BOX:** https://givebackbox.com/works

    What they do: Through their website, you can request a donation box, fill it with unwanted household items such as clothing and shoes, and ship it back to them. They will distribute them to people in need.
    What they need: Any household items, shoes, and clothing.

- [ ] **97. MERCY SHIPS:** https://www.mercyships.org/get-involved/ways-to-give/

    What they do: Mercy Ships uses hospital ships to transform lives and serve nations, one at a time. They provide medical surgeries and treatments.
    What they need: Any form of donations (monetary and volunteers).

- [ ] **98. UCP WHEELS FOR HUMANITY:** https://www.devex.com/organizations/ucpwheels-for-humanity-49373

    What they do: Wheels for Humanity in North Hollywood refurbishes donated wheelchairs for people with disabilities in developing nations through international healthcare partnerships.
    What they need: Any wheelchair and crutches.

- [ ] **99. USED CARD BOXES:** https://www.usedcardboardboxes.com/

    What they do: They buy used containers like gaylords, totes, boxes, and pallets at rates above recycling prices. These items, often used for bulk food and high-volume items, are commonly returned, reused, or resold.
    What they need: Gaylords, produce totes, shipping boxes & other commodities.

- [ ] **100. WOUNDED WARRIORS PROJECT:** https://www.woundedwarriorproject.org/

    What they do: They support veterans and their families through providing variety of veteran programs and services to help them take steps.
    What they need: Any monetary help or volunteer.

INSPIRING QUOTES

"Simplicity is not the opposite of wealth. It is the door to the riches you already own"
- Alan Cotter

"Nature teaches us, simplicity and contentment, because in its presence, we realize we need very little to be happy"
- Mark Colemar

"The greatest gift you can give yourself: YOU have enough, YOU are enough!"
- Rita Wilklins

MEET RITA

Rita Wilkins is a nationally recognized interior design and lifestyle design expert, a TEDx speaker, and author of the best-selling book, "Downsize Your Life, Upgrade Your Lifestyle: Secrets to More Time, Money, and Freedom."

Also known as the "Downsizing Designer," Rita is committed to helping people learn how to declutter and downsize their lives so that they can live a simpler, more abundant life with less.

As a minimalist herself, Rita is passionate about helping others experience the freedom of owning less by going from a life full of excess stuff to a life filled with meaning and purpose.

VISIT RITA AT DESIGNSERVICESLTD.COM

SCAN THE QR CODE BELOW!

Thank you for purchasing Rita's Minimalist Essentials. Visit designservicesltd.com and use this Coupon Code: RITAME to get a 10% discount on Rita's other products

www.ingramcontent.com/pod-product-compliance
Lightning Source LLC
Chambersburg PA
CBHW042354070526
44585CB00028B/2925